Welcoming Spring

by Cara Torrance

OXFORD
UNIVERSITY PRESS
AUSTRALIA & NEW ZEALAND

T0362684

Spring is Here!

People like to celebrate the end of winter and the start of spring. They celebrate in different ways, from eating pancakes to throwing bright powders.

People chase cheese. They watch flowers bloom ...

... and they balance eggs.

Welcoming spring can be a lot of fun!

Pancake Week

Russia

Do you like pancakes? Eating pancakes is one way that people welcome spring.

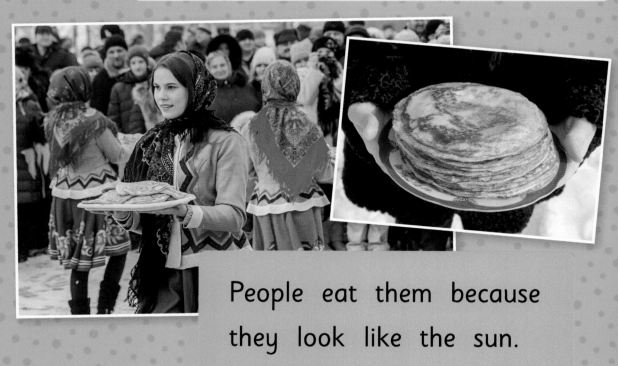

People eat them because they look like the sun.

People sing, visit each other's houses and ride sledges in the snow.

Holi

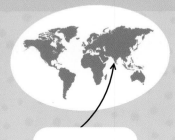

India

Holi is another way that people celebrate spring. They light fires and throw bright powders.

People get covered!

There is a lot of noise, too. People listen to loud music, sing and dance.

Sometimes, people ride their bicycles.

Chasing the Cheese

England

Some people like a **challenge** in spring! At Cooper's Hill in England, they chase a wheel of cheese down the steep hill.

People charge down the hill after the cheese!

Running downhill is hard on the knees! People often fall over, but if they capture the cheese they get to keep it.

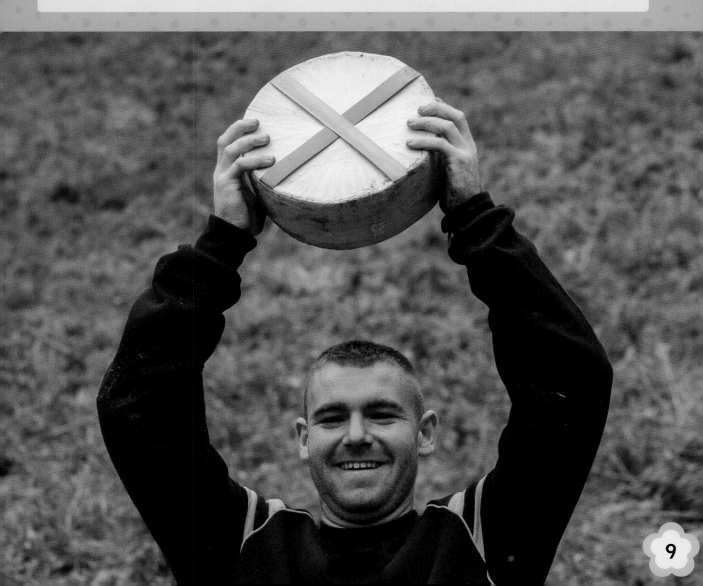

Cherry Blossoms

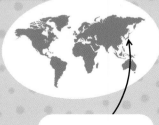

Japan

Blossom on cherry trees is a welcome sign of spring in Japan.

In the past, this was a sign that farmers should plant their rice.

People have picnics under the flowering trees.

People eat, drink and catch up with friends.

Kings Park Flowers

Australia

This **festival** celebrates wild flowers. People visit the park to enjoy the flowers.

The flowers bloom for over a month.

The first Kings Park Festival was held over 50 years ago.

The festival has grown bigger every year.

Lim Festival

Vietnam

At this festival, people welcome spring by singing songs. Singers compete to win a singing **contest**.

Some singers are given money wrapped in red paper or cloth.

Some people play human **chess** with real people acting as the chess pieces.

Breakfast Eggs

Bosnia

Here, people get up at **dawn** and meet by the river on the first day of spring.

Thousands of people enjoy a meal of eggs. Some people go for a swim. They need to be brave as the river is cold!

A Game of Eggs

China

In China, children play the 'egg-standing game'. The challenge is to get an egg to stand up on its end.

It is not easy!

If you can stand an egg on its end,
it is a sign of good luck.

Pyramid Climbing

Mexico

In one part of Mexico, people welcome spring by climbing a giant pyramid.

Thousands of people **gather** to climb the pyramid.

They climb 360 steps up. Once at the top, they take time to enjoy the sun.

These people have climbed to the top of the pyramid.

How would you like to celebrate spring?

looking at flowers

playing chess

standing eggs

climbing pyramids

Glossary

challenge: something that is hard to do

chess: a game of skill with black and white pieces

contest: an event in which people compete

dawn: the time of the day when the sun rises and it gets light

festival: a time when people celebrate something

gather: when people form a group

Index